Seasonal Bulletin Boards

How to Use This Book

- Choose the bulletin board you want to create.

- Read the directions and gather materials. Adjust the design of the board to fit your bulletin board.

- Laminate the full-color caption letters and additional color cutouts. You will find these pages at the back of the book.

- Add your own original touches and student work.

Table of Contents

C

A

B

D

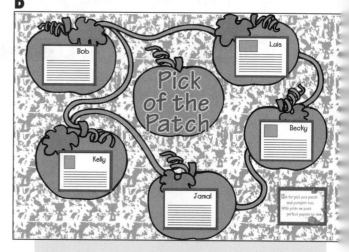

PREVIEW

G

E

F

H

I

Our Bumper Crop

Materials

- background—bright, contrasting solid color paper

- scarecrow:
  arms and shirt—gingham cloth or a plastic checkered tablecloth
  hands—garden gloves
  head—paper plate
  hair—yellow roving or yarn
  hat—9″ x 12″ (23 x 30.5 cm) brown construction paper
  stuffing—cotton stuffing or newspaper

- assorted construction paper for mounting student work

- cutouts:
  caption letters on pages 83 and 85, laminated and trimmed
  crow on page 87, laminated and trimmed

Steps to Follow

1. Cover the bulletin board with background paper. The color you choose will depend on the color of the cloth you use for the scarecrow's shirt. Back the board in a bright contrasting color.

2. Fold the cloth to form long arms. Pin the arms along the top of the board. Fill the arms with crumpled newspaper for dimension. Pin the bottom side of the arms.

3. Lightly stuff the gloves with newspaper. Pin gloves at the end of each arm. Push the gingham sleeves into the gloves.

4. Add felt pen features to the paper plate. Pin the head to the center of the arms.

5. Cut strips of yellow roving or yarn to tie in clumps for hair. Pin to the sides of the paper plate.

6. Cut a hat from brown construction paper. Pin the hat to the top of the head.

7. Pin the caption to the bulletin board.

8. Pin the crow in place.

9. Pin up construction paper sheets to back student work. Add the work.

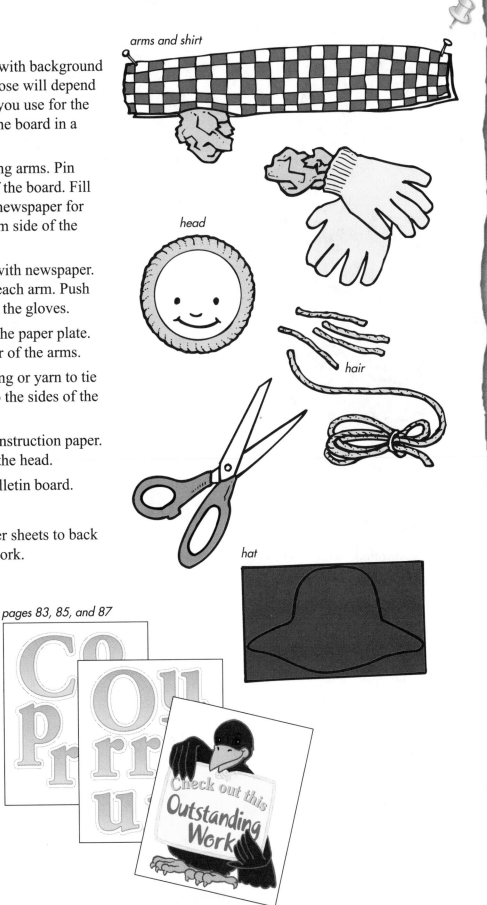

arms and shirt

head

hair

hat

pages 83, 85, and 87

Check out this Outstanding Work

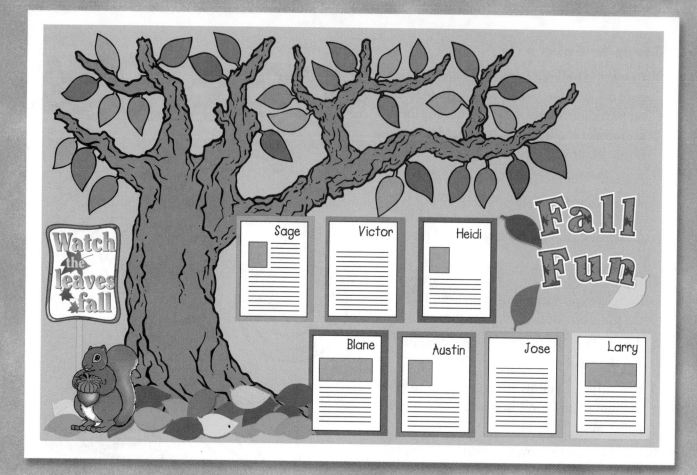

Fall Fun

Materials

- background—natural colored burlap or butcher paper, color of your choice
- tree trunk and branches—brown paper bags
- leaves—green, yellow, orange, and red construction paper
- narrow stick or dowel
- construction paper on which to post student work
- cutouts:
  caption letters on page 89, laminated and trimmed
  squirrel on page 91, laminated and trimmed
  sign on page 93, laminated and trimmed

Steps to Follow

1. Cover the bulletin board area with the burlap or butcher paper.

2. Crumple and twist brown paper bags. Pin the bags to the bulletin board in the shape of a tree trunk and branches. Make the tree as large as your board permits. Why not let it extend over the top of the board?

3. Make the leaves on the tree.

   • Cut leaves from the construction paper. Sandwich a green piece of paper and a colored piece of paper so that you are cutting pairs of leaves the same size.

   • Glue the green leaf and the colored leaf back to back.

   • Pin the leaves to the branches of the tree so that the green sides are showing.

4. Tape the stick on the back of the sign and pin the sign with the squirrel to the bulletin board.

5. Add the caption.

6. Add student writing to the board.

tree trunk

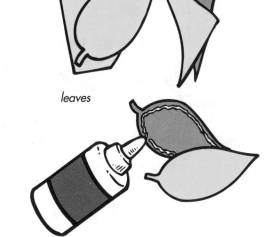

leaves

Each day turn a few leaves from green to their other colored side. Begin to move the colored leaves from the branches to pile up below the tree. After several weeks the tree's branches should be bare. Then fill the branches with samples of student work.

pages 89, 91, and 93

A Is for Awesome!

Materials

- background—white butcher paper
- apple squares—for each square you will need:
  black square—9″ x 9″ (23 x 23 cm)
  red, green, or yellow square—6″ x 6″ (15 x 15 cm)
  white square—5″ x 5″ (13 x 13 cm)
  stem—scraps of brown construction paper
  leaf—scraps of green construction paper
  seeds—black beans
- reproducible apple poem form on page 98
- cutouts:
  caption letters on page 95, laminated and trimmed
  awesome apple on page 97, laminated and trimmed
  sentence strip on page 99, laminated and trimmed

Steps to Follow

1. Cover the bulletin board area with white butcher paper.

2. Use apple squares to form a border. Your students will enjoy making the squares. Follow the steps as shown.

   • Fold red, yellow, or green paper in half. Cut half of an apple shape on the fold.

   • Fold and cut the white paper in the same shape.

   • Glue the white shape on the colored shape.

   • Glue the black beans on the white paper as seeds.

   • Cut a stem from brown and a leaf from green construction paper scraps.

   • Arrange all the pieces on the black square. Glue in place.

3. Add the caption.

4. Add the sentence strip—*Good work comes in many varieties*.

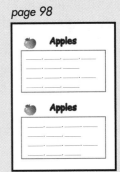

Apple Poems

Write apple poems using the form on page 98 and display them on the board. Taste an apple and make a list of words or phrases that describe how the apple looks, smells, tastes, feels, and sounds.

Use some of the words from your list along with other words in this poem frame. Follow these rules:

• Only one word may be placed in each space.
• Use a word only once.

Crisp	juicy	tart	sweet
Fresh	and	clean	
A	sweet	taste	treat
With	no	caffeine	

page 98

> **Apples**
>
> **Apples**

Post the apple poems on the bulletin board.

Pick of the Patch

Materials

- background—white butcher paper

- brown tempera paint and sponge

- pumpkin patch—per pumpkin:
  leaves—6″ x 6″ (15 x 15 cm) green construction paper
  vines—12″ x 18″ (30.5 x 45.5 cm) green construction paper
  stems—3″ x 3″ (7.5 x 7.5 cm) green construction paper
  tendrils—6″ x 6″ (15 x 15 cm) green construction paper
  pumpkins—12″ x 18″ (30.5 x 45.5 cm) orange construction paper

- cutouts:
  caption letters on pages 101 and 103, laminated and trimmed
  poem on page 105, laminated and trimmed

Steps to Follow

1. Cover the bulletin board area with white butcher paper.

2. Sponge paint the background with brown paint.

3. Make the pumpkin vines.

   • Cut an orange pumpkin for each student.

   • Cut a green stem and leaf for each pumpkin.

   • Write a student's name on each pumpkin.

   • Glue the pumpkin, stem, and leaf together.

4. Pin pumpkins on the bulletin board.

5. Connect the pumpkins with vine strips. Bend and curl the strips to add dimension.

6. Add tendrils.

7. Add the caption and the poem.

8. Post student work on each pumpkin.

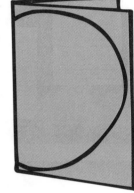

P is for pick and patch
and pumpkin too.
With pride we post
perfect papers to view.

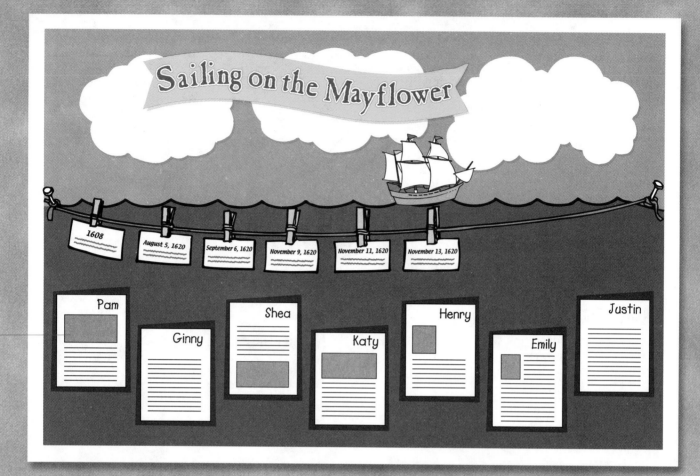

Sailing on the Mayflower

Materials

- background:
  light blue butcher paper for sky
  dark blue butcher paper for water

- banner—6″ x 36″ (15 x 91 cm) yellow butcher paper

- clouds—cotton batting

- time line:
  heavy black roving
  clothespins
  5″ x 8″ (13 x 20 cm) note cards

- cutouts:
  caption letters on pages 107 and 109, laminated and trimmed
  ship on page 111, laminated and trimmed

Steps to Follow

1. Cover the top of the bulletin board area with light blue paper.

2. Cut waves on the top edge of the dark blue paper and pin it to the lower part of the board.

3. Cut clouds from cotton batting and add them to the sky.

4. Cut a banner from the yellow butcher paper. Pin it to the board and add the caption to it.

5. Suspend the black roving across the water.

6. Pin the ship cutout to the left side of the board.

7. Attach the first time line statement to the roving with a clothespin.

8. Move the ship across the time line as you add the statements.

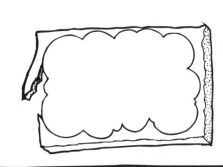

Time Line Statements

Write each event on a note card. Attach the cards to the time line with clothespins.

1608
The Pilgrims leave England and move to the town of Leyden in Holland. There they may worship in the way that they choose. They live there for 12 years before deciding to go to the New World.

August 5, 1620
The *Mayflower* and the *Speedwell* set sail for the New World. The *Speedwell* starts leaking, and the two ships return to shore in England.

September 6, 1620
The *Mayflower* leaves the *Speedwell* behind and sails from Plymouth, England.

November 9, 1620
The Pilgrims reach Cape Cod in what is now Massachusetts.

November 11, 1620
The first party of 16 men from the *Mayflower* go ashore on the tip of Cape Cod to look around and collect firewood.

November 13, 1620
The women of the *Mayflower* go ashore to do the washing.

December 11, 1620
A group of 18 men, Pilgrims and crew from the *Mayflower* exploring in a small boat, land on Plymouth Rock.

December 16, 1620
The *Mayflower* with all the Pilgrims sail to Plymouth and land.

April 5, 1621
Captain Jones and his crew sail the *Mayflower* back to England.

Note: Because England and her colonies did not adopt the presently-used Gregorian calendar until 1752, 10 days must be added to all dates given in Pilgrim records in order to determine the date according to the modern calendar.

Tom Turkey Presents...

Materials

- background—brown package wrapping paper

- turkey:
  body—two 12″ x 18″ (30.5 x 45.5 cm) brown construction paper
  wings—12″ x 18″ (30.5 x 45.5 cm) brown construction paper
  head—9″ x 12″ (23 x 30.5 cm) brown construction paper
  feathers—cut from 4″ x 18″ (10 x 45.5 cm) red, yellow, and orange construction paper
  legs—two 12″ x 18″ (30.5 x 45.5 cm) black construction paper
  eyes—2 black beads
  beak—yellow construction paper scrap
  wattle—red construction paper scrap

- 4 file folder strips—2″ x 9″ (5 x 23 cm)

- yarn

- cutouts:
  caption letters on pages 113 and 115, laminated and trimmed
  sign on page 115, laminated and trimmed
  Pilgrim hat on page 117, laminated and trimmed

Steps to Follow

1. Cover the bulletin board area with the brown wrapping paper.

2. Make the turkey.

   • Tape two of the pieces of 12″ x 18″ brown construction paper together. Cut a circle for the body of the turkey. Pin the circle to the bulletin board.

   • Have each student trim and fringe feathers from the orange, yellow, and red construction paper.

   • Pin the feathers to the board. Do not make them flat. Pin them so that they are rippled.

   • Cut a smaller circle from the 9″ x 12″ piece of brown paper for the turkey's head. Add a yellow beak and a red wattle. Add black beads for eyes. Put the Pilgrim's hat on the turkey.

   • Make two catstair springs from the file folder strips as shown. Tape one end of one spring to the turkey's body and the other end to the back of the turkey's head.

   • Make another spring and tape one end to the back of the hat and the other end to the bulletin board.

   • Fold the remaining piece of 12″ x 18″ brown paper in half. Cut out the wings and pin them on the turkey.

   • Cut out black construction paper legs and pin in place.

3. Add the caption.

4. Punch holes in the sign and tie a piece of yarn to each end. Hang it around the turkey's neck.

5. Add student work.

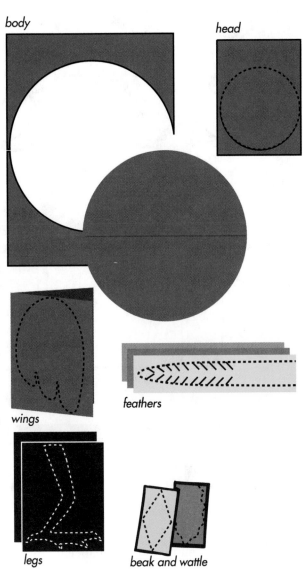

body

head

wings

feathers

legs

beak and wattle

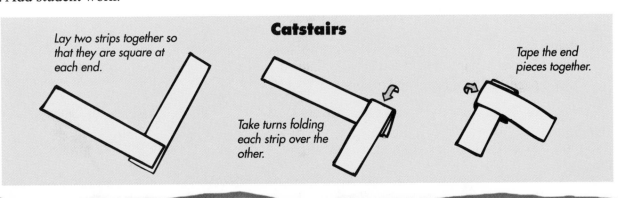

Catstairs

Lay two strips together so that they are square at each end.

Take turns folding each strip over the other.

Tape the end pieces together.

Where we walk to school each day
Indian children used to play—
What a different place today
Where we live and work and play!

If I Were a Native American...

Materials

- background—purple butcher paper

- Native American children:
  face—6" x 6" (15 x 15 cm) manila paper
  hands—3" x 3" (7.5 x 7.5 cm) manila paper
  torso—9" x 12" (23 x 30.5 cm) brown construction paper
  feathers and headbands—scraps of colorful construction paper
  hair—black yarn
  pants—brown lunch bags and 2" x 12" (5 x 30.5 cm) strips of orange construction paper
  brown construction paper on which to display student work

- cutouts:
  caption letters on pages 119, 121, and 123, laminated and trimmed
  sign on page 123, laminated and trimmed

Steps to Follow

1. Cover the bulletin board area with the purple paper.

2. Make the children.

   • Cut heads from the manila paper.

   • Draw faces and add yarn hair. Add headbands and feathers cut from construction paper. Decorate the headbands with beads or paper scraps.

   • Cut out small circles for hands.

   • Make pants and moccasins from the brown paper bags. Draw a center line with a marking pen. Add orange fringe to each side. Cut bottom flap to form moccasins as shown.

3. Pin the children to the board.

   • First, the heads in a row…

   • Next, rectangles of brown construction paper…

   • Pin hands holding the rectangles…

   • Finally, the paper bag pants and moccasins.

4. Add the caption and sign.

5. Post student work on the brown rectangles.

head

hands

hair

pants

page 123

Where we walk to school each day
Indian children used to play—
What a different place today
Where we live and work and play!

Indian Children

Where we walk to school each day
Indian children used to play—
All about our native land,
Where the shops and houses stand.

And the trees were very tall,
And there were no streets at all,
Not a church and not a steeple—
Only woods and Indian people.

Only wigwams on the ground,
And at night bears prowling round—
What a different place today
Where we live and work and play!

by Annette Wynne, Copyright 1919

Popping With Good Ideas

Materials

- background—blue butcher paper

- popcorn popper:
  silver posterboard
  black construction paper
  yarn or roving

- popcorn—12″ x 18″ (30.5 x 45.5 cm) white construction paper

- cutouts:
  caption letters on page 125, laminated and trimmed
  sign on page 127, laminated and trimmed
  "Pop" bursts on page 129, laminated and trimmed

Steps to Follow

1. Cover the bulletin board area with blue butcher paper.

2. Make the popcorn popper.

   • Cut the shape from the silver posterboard.

   • Cut a handle and plug from black construction paper as shown.

   • Cut roving as the cord. Tape one end to the back of the popper and the other end to the plug.

3. Pin the popper to the board.

4. Cut large pieces of white paper in the shapes of popped kernels. Pin the kernels around the popper.

5. Add the caption, sign, and the "pop" bursts.

6. Post student work on the popped kernels.

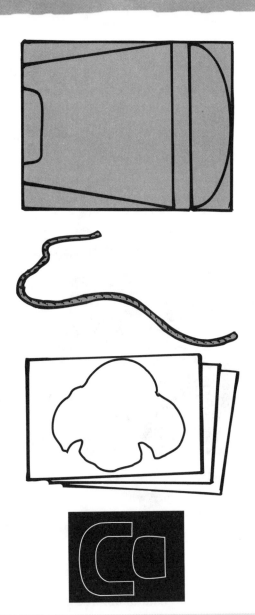

Why does popcorn pop?

Native American folklore told of spirits who lived inside each kernel of popcorn. The spirits were quiet and content to live on their own—but grew angry if their houses were heated. The hotter their homes became, the angrier they'd get—shaking the kernels until the heat was too much. Finally they would burst out of their homes and into the air as a disgruntled puff of steam.

All seeds contain a tiny bit of water whose job is to keep cells alive until sprouting. This small amount of moisture makes the popping of popcorn possible. When a kernel of popcorn is heated, the water inside becomes a gas (steam) that exerts a strong enough pressure to burst the seed covering. The expansion of the gas causes an explosion. The soft starch inside the kernel becomes inflated and bursts, turning it inside out. The steam inside the kernel is released, and the popcorn is popped!

A Harvest of Excellence

Materials

- background—natural colored burlap
- cornucopia:
  brown wrapping paper
  dark brown construction paper 12″ x 18″ (30.5 x 45.5 cm)
- colored leaves on page 135 and additional leaves cut from brightly-colored construction paper
- construction paper for mounting student work
- cutouts:
  caption letters on pages 131 and 133, laminated and trimmed

Steps to Follow

1. Cover the bulletin board area with burlap.

2. Cut an oval shape from the 12″ x 18″ brown construction paper. Pin the oval to the board. This forms the inside of your cornucopia.

3. Crumple brown wrapping paper and pin to the bulletin board around one side of the oval to form the cornucopia.

4. Cut out the colored leaves on page 135. Cut additional leaves as needed from brightly-colored construction paper. Pin them spilling out of the cornucopia.

5. Add the caption.

6. Add student work framed with construction paper in various fall colors.

page 135

Variations for Using Your Cornucopia

• Display photos of your students mounted on the colorful leaves spilling from the cornucopia. Add a handwritten note about each student noting a special achievement or why you are thankful to know that student.

• Have students write tributes to special people in your school. Post the tributes with photos or drawings in the cornucopia.

WINTER

C

The Year of the Super Student

2001

A

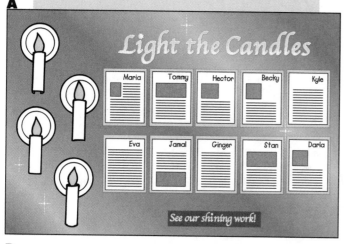

Light the Candles

| Maria | Tommy | Hector | Becky | Kyle |

| Eva | Jamal | Ginger | Stan | Darla |

See our shining work!

D

Winter Winners

Well-done   Wonderful

Worthy

B

December Celebrations

Christmas   Las Posadas

Kwanzaa   Hanukkah

How do You Celebrate?

PREVIEW

G

H

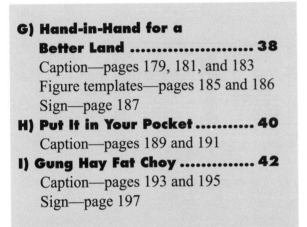

F

I

Seasonal Bulletin Boards • EMC 786

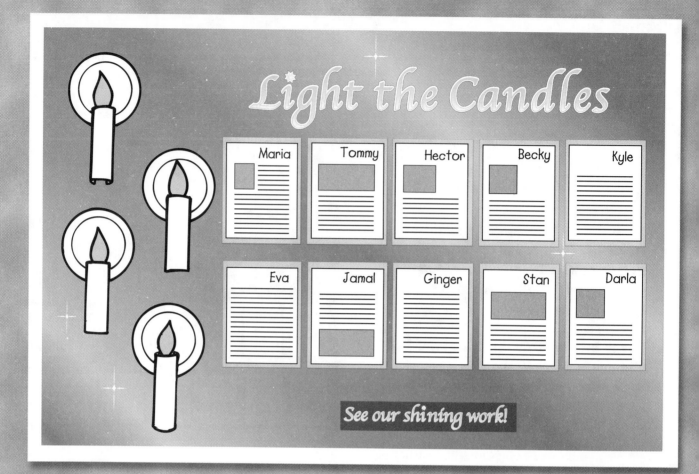

Light the Candles

Materials

- background—shiny foil wrapping paper
- candles:
  candlestick—6″ x 8″ (15 x 20 cm) white posterboard
  flame—5″ x 3″ (13 x 7.5 cm) yellow construction paper
  reflector—four 8″ (20 cm) paper plates
  spray glitter
- 9″ x 12″ (23 x 30.5 cm) construction paper for mounting student work
- cutouts:
  caption letters on pages 137 and 139, laminated and trimmed
  sentence strip on page 141, laminated and trimmed

Steps to Follow

1. Cover the bulletin board area with the shiny wrapping paper.

2. Make the candles.

   • Cut flames from yellow construction paper as shown. Glue the flame to the paper plate.

   • Cut rectangles from the posterboard.

   • Fold under a narrow flap on each side.

   • Pin the flaps to the board along with the paper plate so that the rectangle forms a rounded candle.

   • Pin the paper plate at the top of the candle.

   • Spray glitter on the flame and the candle.

3. Add the caption and the sentence strip.

4. Post student work on colored construction paper.

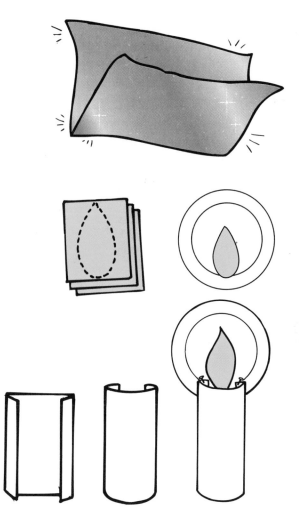

Interesting Connections

The candles on this bulletin board may be used in many different ways. Here are just two examples of the ways you might use them to initiate class discussion and writing.

• Eleanor Roosevelt once said, "If each person would light just one little candle, we could light the darkness." Discuss with your class what Mrs. Roosevelt might have meant by *darkness*. Then document the candles that your students have lit.

• A candle left burning in the window marked a station in the Underground Railroad. Imagine with your students how it might have felt to approach a house and decide whether to knock on the door.

December Celebrations

Materials

- background—blue butcher paper
- reproducible writing form on page 154
- 5" x 11" (13 x 28 cm) construction paper in colors shown for mounting holiday signs
- cutouts:
  caption letters on pages 143, 145, and 147, laminated and trimmed
  pictures on page 147, laminated and trimmed
  holiday signs on pages 149 and 151, laminated and trimmed
  December calendar form on page 153, laminated and trimmed

Steps to Follow

1. Cover the bulletin board with blue butcher paper.

2. Add the caption letters across the top.

3. Write numbers on the December calendar form and pin it on the board.

4. Cut out the holiday signs from pages 149 and 151 and the pictures from page 147, and glue them to the colored construction paper. Pin them to the board.

5. Add the writing forms the students have completed.

Celebrating Las Posadas

In Mexico, beginning on December 16 and for the next nine nights, Posadas processions reenact Mary and Joseph's search for lodging in Bethlehem. A parade of children carrying lanterns and platforms with figures of Mary and Joseph stop at homes of neighbors and beg to be taken in. When they reach a prearranged house, the manger is carried in, prayers said, and refreshments served. A piñata is often the highlight of the party.

Celebrating Hanukkah

People celebrate Hanukkah to remember a miracle. Judah, the Maccabee, fought the Syrians for three years. When he and his men finally defeated the Syrians, they reclaimed their temple. The temple was cleaned, and the Jewish soldiers relit the Lamp of Eternal Light. They had only enough oil for one day, but the oil lasted for eight days, until the new oil arrived.

Hanukkah begins on the twenty-fifth day of the Jewish month of Kislev and it lasts for eight days. During Hanukkah, families gather every night to light the menorah. Traditional foods served during the celebration include potato pancakes, called *latkes*, and applesauce. Children receive small gifts on each of the eight nights and play with a square-sided top called a *dreidel*.

Celebrating Christmas

Christmas is a celebration of the birth of Jesus. On December 25, Christians around the world celebrate His birth with the giving of gifts, singing of carols, and family gatherings. In Spain, children believe that three wise men bring them gifts. In Russia, a good witch named Babouska sneaks into houses to slip gifts under children's pillows. Swedish children wait for Jultomten, a present-giving elf, while German children place baskets by their front doors so that the Christkindl will fill them with cookies and candy. American children hang stockings by the chimney on Christmas Eve, hoping for a visit from Santa Claus. In England, Santa is called Father Christmas. Polish children wait for the Star Man, and in France, Pere Noel brings presents to children on Christmas Day.

Celebrating Kwanzaa

Kwanzaa is a Swahili word that means "first fruits." This holiday was begun in 1966 to celebrate African-American heritage. Families celebrate Kwanzaa for seven days. They light candles in a special candleholder called a *kinara*. Each day of Kwanzaa has a special meaning or principle. At the end of the seven days, children receive handmade gifts. Families and friends enjoy a feast, sing songs, play music, and share stories of their heritage.

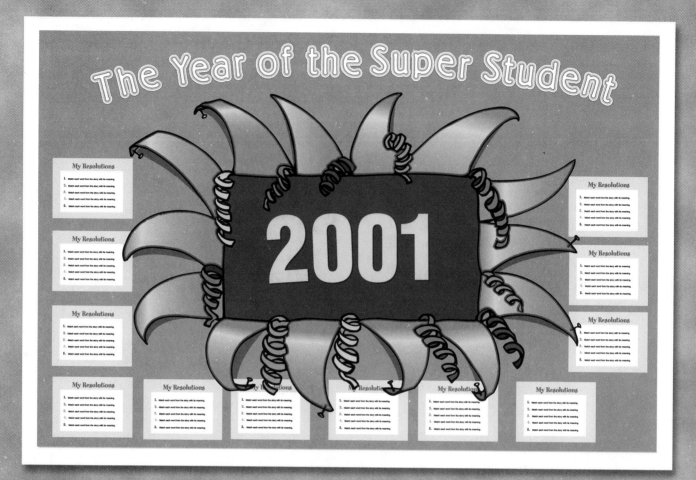

 # The Year of the Super Student

Materials

- background:
  dark colored butcher paper or foil wrapping paper
  bright colored butcher paper

- 2001 numbers—four 9″ x 12″ (23 x 30.5 cm) yellow construction paper

- narrow streamers in bright colors

- cutouts:
  caption letters on pages 155, 157, and 159, laminated and trimmed

Steps to Follow

1. Staple a rectangle of the dark paper in the center of the bulletin board.

2. Cover the whole board with the bright paper. Starting from the center, cut diagonal lines out. Roll the resulting flaps back. Pin in place.

3. Make construction paper numbers for the new year.

4. Pin the numbers to the exposed area in the center of the board.

5. Pin streamers spilling out of the center and spreading out across the board.

6. Add the caption.

7. Post student resolutions around the edge of the board.

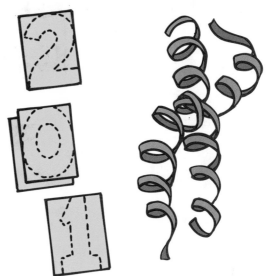

New Year's Resolutions

A New Year's resolution is a promise to improve or try to make something happen during the upcoming year. Try writing this special resolution. Have students describe the person that they want to be.

- Students list five or six things that they want to do in the upcoming year.

  ride a bike   make a quilt   get a puppy   sing a solo

- Students write a resolution using this format:

  This year I'm going to be a

      bike-riding,

      quilt-making,

      puppy-owning,

      solo-singing,

      super student!

Winter Winners

Materials

- background—blue butcher paper

- mitten:
  red felt, cloth, or butcher paper
  white batting or butcher paper

- mouse:
  head—12″ x 18″ (30.5 x 45.5 cm) gray construction paper
  nose—3″ x 3″ (7.5 x 7.5 cm) pink construction paper
  scarf—12″ x 3″ (30.5 x 7.5 cm) yellow construction paper

- snowflakes:
  squares of white copy paper

- cutouts:
  caption letters on pages 161 and page 163, laminated and trimmed
  word strips on pages 163 and 165, laminated and trimmed

Steps to Follow

1. Cover the bulletin board area with blue butcher paper.

2. Make the mitten.

   • Cut the shape from the red material or butcher paper.

   • Pin the mitten in place.

   • Cut a cuff of the white batting or paper and pin it on the mitten.

3. Cut snowflakes and pin randomly around mitten.

4. Cut the mouse from gray construction paper as shown. Add details with a marking pen. Pin the mouse so that it is peeking out of the mitten. Add the scarf, fringed on the edges.

5. Add the caption. Scatter the word strips around the board and pin on the snowflakes.

6. Post student work on the mitten.

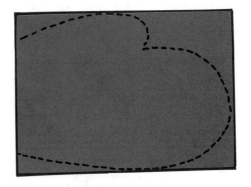

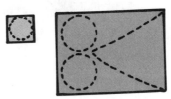

Snowflakes

How to cut a simplified snowflake.

Sweet Winter Dreams

Materials

- background—dark blue butcher paper
- bear:
  body—12″ x 18″ (30.5 x 45.5 cm) brown construction paper
  arms, head, ears—12″ x 18″ (30.5 x 45.5 cm) brown construction paper
  legs—9″ x 12″ (23 x 30.5 cm) brown construction paper
  muzzle, inner ears—6″ x 9″ (15 x 23 cm) beige construction paper
  nose—2″ x 2½″ (5 x 6.5 cm) black construction paper
- dream clouds—white butcher paper
- contrasting color construction paper for mounting student work
- cutouts:
  caption letters on pages 167 and 169, laminated and trimmed
  stars on page 171, laminated and trimmed

Steps to Follow

1. Cover the bulletin board area with dark blue butcher paper.

2. Make the sleeping bear.

   • Cut the shapes from construction paper.

   • Glue the shapes together.

   • Add details with a marking pen:
     eyes
     mouth

   • Pin the bear in place.

3. Cut dream clouds from white butcher paper. Pin the clouds in place.

4. Add the caption.

5. Add the star cutouts.

6. Post student work on colored construction paper.

body

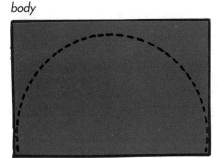

head, outer ears, arms

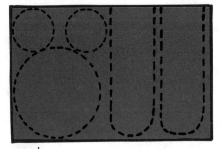

muzzle, inner ears   *legs*

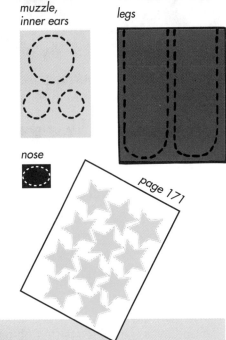

nose

page 171

A Good Book

There are great books available about hibernating animals. Read several as you introduce your new bulletin board. Here are five good picture books:

A Bed for Winter by Karen Wallace; Dorling Kindersley, 2000.

Every Autumn Comes the Bear by Jim Arnosky; Putnam Publishing, 1996.

Time to Sleep by Denise Fleming; Henry Holt and Company, 1997.

The Valentine Bears by Eve Bunting; Clarion Books, 1995.

What Will I Do Without You? by Sally Grindley; Larousse Kingfisher Chambers, 1999.

A Blizzard of Good Work

Materials

- background—dark blue butcher paper

- snowman:
  light blue butcher paper
  buttons—yellow construction paper
  scarf—red construction paper
  nose—orange construction paper
  hat and eyes—black construction paper
  arms—thin twigs

- white tempera paint and sponge

- snowflakes:
  white construction paper squares

- construction paper for mounting student work

- cutouts:
  caption letters on pages 173, 175, and 177, laminated and trimmed

Steps to Follow

1. Cover the bulletin board area with dark blue butcher paper.

2. Build the snowman:

   • Cut the three snowballs from light blue paper and sponge paint them using the white tempera paint. Let the shapes dry completely.

   • Pin the shapes to the board.

   • Add the scarf, hat, carrot nose, eyes, and buttons cut from construction paper as shown.

   • Pin the twig arms in place.

3. Make snowflakes and pin them across the bottom of the board and around the snowman. Follow the folding and cutting steps shown on page 33.

4. Add the caption.

5. Post student work on the construction paper.

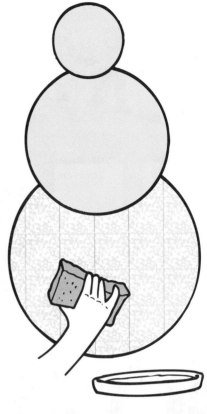

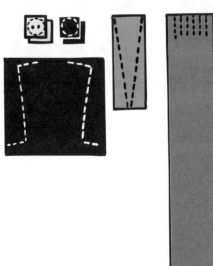

Couplets

Write couplets with your class about a snowman or a snowy day. Display the couplets on the board.

Nibble, nibble, nibble, crunch

This snowman's nose is a bunny's lunch!

Hand-in-Hand for a Better Land

Materials

- background:
  light blue butcher paper
  green butcher paper

- people:
  9″ x 12″ (23 x 30.5 cm) red, brown, yellow, black, and manila construction paper

- cutouts:
  caption letters on pages 179, 181, and 183, laminated and trimmed
  figure templates on pages 185 and 186
  signs on pages 183 and 187, laminated and trimmed

Steps to Follow

1. Cover the top of the bulletin board area with light blue butcher paper.

2. Cut a curve of green butcher paper to represent the horizon and pin it to the bottom two thirds of the board.

3. Create people.

   • Trace the people templates on brown, red, yellow, black, and manila construction paper. Cut out enough people to stretch across the top of the green curved paper.

   • Pin the people to the board so that they appear to be standing hand-in-hand.

4. Add the caption. Also pin up the sign about Martin Luther King and his contributions.

5. Post student work.

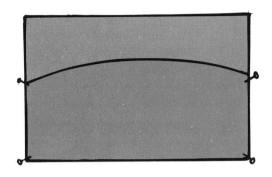

page 183

page 187

He Changed America

Martin Luther King

Use the celebration of Martin Luther King, Jr.'s birthday as a chance for meaningful writing. Here are two ideas to get you started:

• What does it mean to stand "hand-in-hand"? Have your students tell about a time when they stood together for a common belief or cause. How did standing hand-in-hand make a difference?

• Martin Luther King, Jr. had a dream that all people would be judged by the content of their character and not the color of their skin. Have students write about what makes up a person's character.

Put It in Your Pocket

Materials

- background—white butcher paper

- pockets:
  12″ x 18″ (30.5 x 45.5 cm) red construction paper
  6″ x 6″ (15 x 15 cm) pink construction paper

- heart bugs:
  4″ x 4″ (10 x 10 cm) pink construction paper squares
  scraps of ribbon, lace, and wrapping paper
  tongue depressor sticks
  short strips of pipe cleaners
  red crayons or markers

- cutouts:
  caption letters on pages 189 and 191, laminated and trimmed

Steps to Follow

1. Cover the bulletin board with white butcher paper.

2. Make the pockets.

   • Fold the red paper up 6″ to form a pocket. Staple the sides.

   • Hold the pink square and cut around the thumb to create a half heart.

   • Lay the pink cut-out square in the bottom left corner of the pocket and glue it in place as shown.

   • Glue the half heart, that has been cut out, on the opposite side as shown.

   • Print a student's name on each pocket.

3. Add the caption.

4. Make heart bugs with students to pin around the edge of the board.

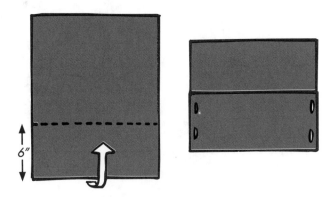

Heart Bugs

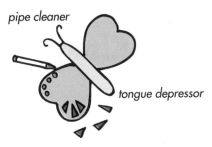

pipe cleaner

tongue depressor

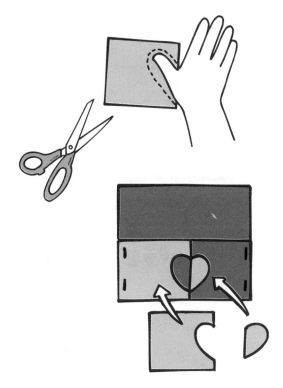

5. Put student work to be displayed in the pockets.

What's In the Pocket?

• Use your pockets as mailboxes for valentine deliveries.

• Put students' work on display.

• Use pockets to hold stories about valentine traditions.

Gung Hay Fat Choy

Materials

- background—red butcher paper

- dragon:
  body—green butcher paper
  ears and mane—green butcher paper
  head—green butcher paper
  eyes, horns, teeth—12″ x 18″ (30.5 x 45.5 cm) yellow construction paper
  nostrils—5″ x 5″ (13 x 13 cm) red construction paper
  tail strips—brightly-colored tissue paper strips

- cutouts:
  caption letters on pages 193 and 195, laminated and trimmed
  Chinese Zodiac Signs on page 197

Seasonal Bulletin Boards • EMC 786

Steps to Follow

1. Cover the bulletin board with red butcher paper.

2. Create the dragon's head out of the green butcher paper. Cut out the red and yellow construction paper as shown to create eyes, nostrils, horns, and teeth. Add a mouth with a marking pen.

3. Make the body of the dragon and attach it to the head.

4. Attach the whole creature to the upper edge of the board. It is nice if the dragon extends above the board and the tail hangs beyond the edge. Attach the tissue paper tail strips.

5. Pin the caption letters to the board along with student work samples.

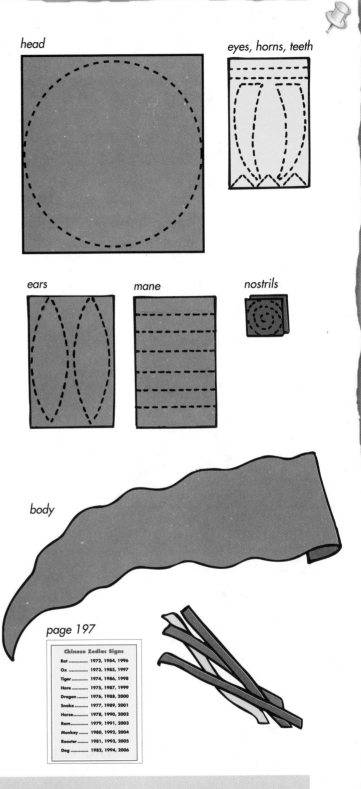

head

eyes, horns, teeth

ears

mane

nostrils

body

page 197

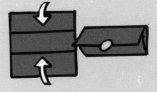

Chinese Zodiac Signs	
Rat	1972, 1984, 1996
Ox	1973, 1985, 1997
Tiger	1974, 1986, 1998
Hare	1975, 1987, 1999
Dragon	1976, 1988, 2000
Snake	1977, 1989, 2001
Horse	1978, 1990, 2002
Ram	1979, 1991, 2003
Monkey	1980, 1992, 2004
Rooster	1981, 1993, 2005
Dog	1982, 1994, 2006

Chinese Zodiac Signs

Have students discover under which sign they were born. They can write the information on a small red piece of paper and fold it. Use a yellow sticker to hold it closed.

SPRING

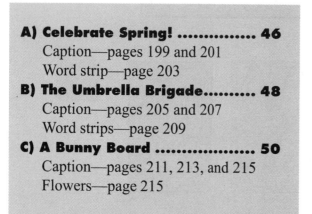

PREVIEW

G

H

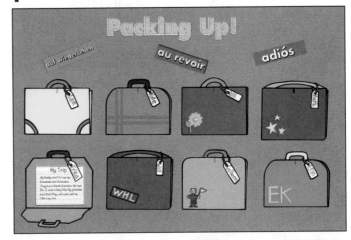

E

F

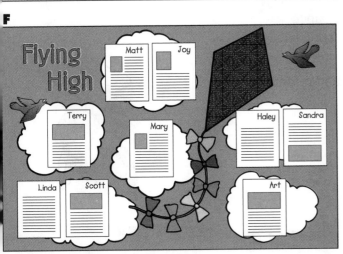

I

45

Celebrate Spring!

Materials

- background—white butcher paper

- rainbow:
  red, orange, yellow, green, medium blue, very dark blue, purple tempera paint, and a sponge

- flowers (for each flower):
  daffodil—12″ x 18″ (30.5 x 45.5 cm) yellow construction paper
  daisy—12″ x 12″ (30.5 x 30.5 cm) pink construction paper
          6″ x 6″ (15 x 15 cm) yellow construction paper
  tulip—12″ x 12″ (30.5 x 30.5 cm) purple construction paper

- cutouts:
  caption letters on pages 199 and 201, laminated and trimmed
  sentence strip on page 203, laminated and trimmed

Steps to Follow

1. Cover the bulletin board area with white butcher paper.

2. Paint the rainbow.

   • Lightly sketch the rainbow lines on the board.

   • Dab paint on each strip of the rainbow with the sponge.

3. Cut the flowers from construction paper as shown. Pin them to the side of the bulletin board.

4. Add the caption and the sentence strip.

5. Post student work on the rainbow.

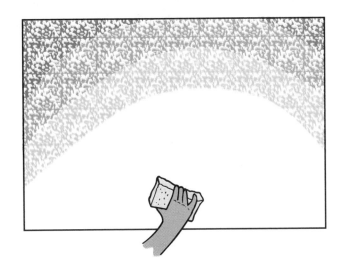

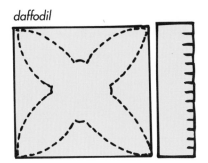

daffodil

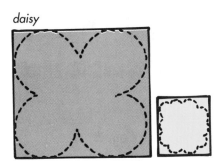

daisy

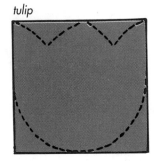

tulip

Chant for Spring

Write a chant or a cheer for spring. Post it on the bulletin board. Read it aloud with feeling.

> Sunny days, sunny days,
> Bright, bold, squinty rays.
> Sunny day, sunny day,
> It's time for us to play.

The Umbrella Brigade

Materials

- background—gray or white butcher paper
- puddle—cellophane wrap or light blue butcher paper
- crayon-resist umbrellas:
  white drawing paper—9″ x 12″ (23 x 30.5 cm)
  watercolor paints
  crayons
- boots:
  shiny wrapping paper or colored construction paper—9″ x 12″ (23 x 30.5 cm)
- cutouts:
  caption letters on pages 205 and 207, laminated and trimmed
  word strips on pages 207 and 209, laminated and trimmed

Steps to Follow

1. Cover the bulletin board with gray or white paper.

2. Make the puddle. Cut a large irregularly shaped puddle for the center of the board.

3. Cut out drops of the puddle material and pin them around the board.

4. Have each student make a crayon-resist umbrella.

   • Cut an umbrella from the white drawing paper.

   • Color a design on the umbrella with crayons.

   • Give the umbrella a watercolor wash.

5. Cut pairs of boots as shown from colorful construction paper.

6. Glue the boots to the bottom of the umbrella.

7. Post the umbrellas and boots in a long line marching onto the bulletin board, across the top, and off the other side.

8. Add the caption and word strips.

9. Display student work on the puddle.

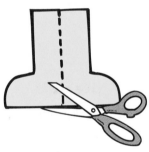

Sing a Chorus

Form a real umbrella brigade and splash through puddles as you recite the lines of this poem:

> "...Let it rain
> Tree-toads and frogs,
> Muskets and pitchforks,
> Kittens and dogs!
>
> Dash away! Plash away!
> Who is afraid?
> Here we go,
> The Umbrella Brigade!"

The chorus of the poem "The Umbrella Brigade" is by Laura E. Richards.

A Bunny Board

Materials

- background—bright green and bright blue butcher paper

- bunnies:
  body, head, and ears—9″ x 12″ (23 x 30.5 cm) white construction paper
  eyes—black beads
  nose and ear centers—6″ x 9″ (15 x 23 cm) pink construction paper
  whiskers—black construction paper scraps
  tail—cotton

- cutouts:
  caption cards on pages 211, 213, and 215, laminated and trimmed
  flowers on page 215, laminated and trimmed

Steps to Follow

1. Cover the top of the bulletin board area with a strip of bright blue butcher paper. Cover the rest of the board with the bright green paper. Fringe the top edge of the green paper to create grass.

2. Make the bunnies with the students.
   - Cut the white paper in half.
   - Cut the head and ears from one piece.
   - Cut the body from the other piece.
   - Cut a pink oval for the nose and pink centers for ears.
   - Add black beads for the eyes.
   - Cut whiskers from black construction paper scraps and glue next to the nose.

3. Add the caption to the bottom of the board.

4. Post student work on the green grass.

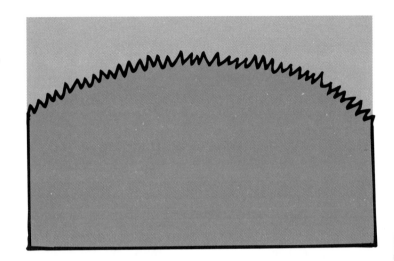

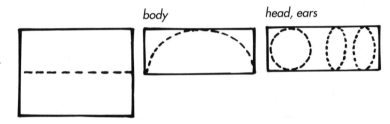

body

head, ears

ear centers, nose

whiskers

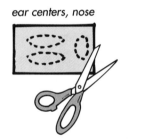

Peter Rabbit

- Read *The Tale of Peter Rabbit* by Beatrix Potter; Dover Publications, 1972. Students will be interested to know that Beatrix Potter wrote stories about Peter Rabbit for a young friend who was sick.

- Recite a poem.

    Naughty little Peter in MacGregor's peas,

    You almost fooled the farmer until he heard you sneeze.

    Hurry home to Mother. Next time use your head.

    Don't go in the garden, go "berrying" instead.

April Showers Bring May Flowers

Materials

- background—light blue butcher paper and green tissue paper
- cloud—white butcher paper
- raindrops and flowers—8½″ x 8½″ (21.5 x 21.5 cm) squares of copy paper
- sun—8″ x 8″ (20 x 20 cm) yellow construction paper
- wooden paint stirrer
- blue marking pen
- cutouts:
  caption letters and ladybugs on pages 217 and 219, laminated and trimmed
  sign on page 221, laminated and trimmed

Steps to Follow

1. Cover the bulletin board with light blue butcher paper.

2. Fringe strips of green tissue paper and add them to the bottom of the board to create a green grass border.

3. Cut a cloud from white butcher paper and pin it to the board.

4. Cut a sun from the yellow construction paper square and tuck it behind the cloud with only a little bit showing.

5. Make dotted rain lines with a blue marker.

6. Have each student make one or two raindrop/flowers for the board.

   • Fold the square of paper.

   • Trim off the tip.

   • Unfold the paper and use marking pens to create a flower on the inside of the raindrop shape.

   • Refold the raindrop and pin it on the board.

7. Pin the caption to the board.

8. Tape the sign to the paint stirrer and position it on the grass. Add the ladybugs.

9. Every few days, move a few raindrops down to the grass and open them up to show the flower inside. By the end of the month all the raindrops should have landed in the grass and blossomed into flowers. The sun can move into full view as the month draws to an end.

10. Display spring stories and poems on the board.

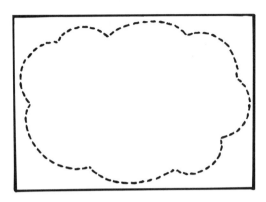

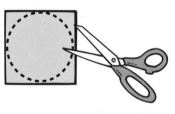

Raining Poetry

Rain, rain, go away.
Come again some other day.

What size is the rain?
 Is it a mist that's barely wet?
 Or merely a sprinkle at sunset?
 Is it a drop? A plop in the mud?
 A downpour? A deluge? A flood?
What size is the rain?

"Eggs"-citing!

Materials

- background—blue butcher paper

- egg:
  white butcher paper
  shredded cellophane

- chicks—4½" x 6" (11.5 x 15 cm) yellow construction paper and orange paper scraps
  black beads for eyes

- brightly-colored construction paper to frame student work

- cutouts:
  caption letters on pages 223 and 227, laminated and trimmed
  sentence strips on pages 225 and 227, laminated and trimmed

Steps to Follow

1. Cover the bulletin board with blue butcher paper. Add the caption and the sentence strips.

2. Make a giant egg from white butcher paper as shown. The size of the egg that you make will depend on the size of your board.

3. Pin the egg to the board.
   Note: Leave the egg in the center of the board for several days. Encourage curiosity about what could be inside the egg. Then complete these steps:

   • While students are home, cut the egg in half, leaving a zig-zag edge, and pin the two pieces to the board.

   • Pin bits of shredded cellophane to the board, spilling out of the egg.

4. Have students make chicks to pin around the board.

5. Display student work.

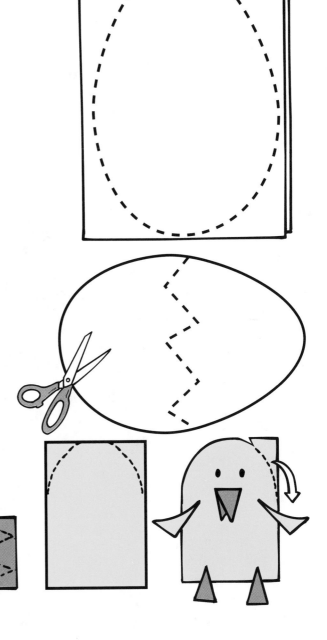

feet

beak

Oviparous

Use your bulletin board as an excuse to learn a great new word—*oviparous*! Oviparous creatures lay eggs. Be sure to read *Chickens Aren't the Only Ones* by Ruth Heller; Putnam Publishing, 1994.

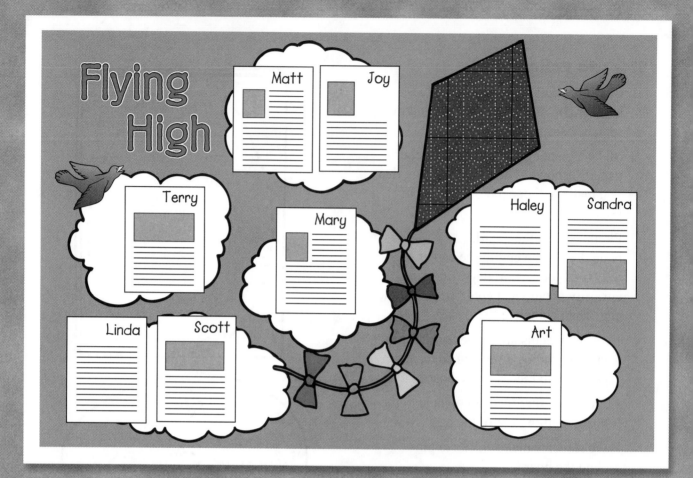

Flying High

Materials

- background—orange butcher paper

- clouds—white tissue paper

- kite:
  colorful wrapping paper
  heavy string or roving
  colorful tissue paper strips

- cutouts:
  caption letters on page 229 and 231, laminated and trimmed
  birds on page 233, laminated and trimmed

Steps to Follow

1. Cover the bulletin board with the butcher paper. You may want a traditional blue sky, but this board is eye-catching done in orange!

2. Cut cloud shapes from the white tissue paper. Crumple the shapes. Smooth them out and pin them to the board.

3. Cut a kite from the wrapping paper. Laminate it before you pin it to the board. Add a string tail.

4. Take the colorful tissue paper strips and twist them in the middle to make ribbons on the tail of the kite.

5. Pin the caption letters to the board.

6. Pin the birds to the board.

7. Pin student work to the clouds.

Write About the Wind

Take a walk on a windy day.

Feel the air as it swirls around you.

Smell and taste the breeze.

When you go back inside, collect your observations. Write words and phrases that tell about the wind.

A Carp for Luck

Materials

- background—bright yellow butcher paper

- long roll of brown butcher paper

- crayon-resist fish kites:
  body—12″ x 18″ (30.5 x 45.5 cm) white drawing paper
  mouth—1″ x 8″ (2.5 x 20 cm) strips of posterboard
  tail—1″ x 6″ (2.5 x 15 cm) tissue paper strips in a variety of colors
  string
  crayons
  watercolors
  hole punch

- colorful construction paper 9″ x 12″ (23 x 30.5 cm) to frame student work

- cutouts:
  caption letters on pages 235 and 237, laminated and trimmed
  sign on page 239

Steps to Follow

1. Cover the bulletin board with yellow butcher paper.

2. Pin the caption on the board.

3. Make a long, tight roll of brown butcher paper for the kite pole. Attach it to one edge of your bulletin board.

4. Have each student make a fish kite.

   • Fold the paper in half.

   • Draw a fish on the paper—the mouth must be at one end and the tail at the other.

   • Color a design on the fish—the more detail the better.

   • Brush the fish all over with watercolor paints.

   • Let the fish dry completely.

   • Staple along the edge of the fish. Leave the mouth and tail open.

   • Glue strips of tissue paper to the inside of the tail.

   • Make a ring of posterboard and slip it inside the fish's mouth. Staple it in place. Punch two holes through the ring.

   • Tie a string through the holes.

5. Hang the kites from the pole, attached with string. Pin the kites to the board as if they were flying in the breeze.

6. Pin the sign telling about Children's Day under the caption.

7. Post student work.

butcher paper roll

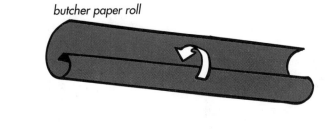

fish kites

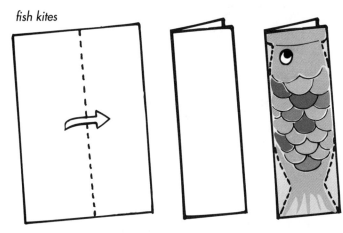

page 239

Children's Day
(Kodomo no hi)

Children's Day is a national holiday in Japan dedicated to celebrating the health and happiness of all children. It falls on May 5. Families put up fish kites, one for each child, symbolizing the wish that their children grow up strong like the carp that swims against the current.

Congratulations, Graduates!

Materials

- background—bright yellow butcher paper

- graduate:
  robe—black butcher paper
  face and hands—light brown construction paper
  shoes—white construction paper
  hair—yarn (your choice of color)
  mortarboard—black construction paper and strips of yarn (your school colors)
  diploma—white copy paper

- cutouts:
  caption letters on pages 241, 243, and 245, laminated and trimmed
  reproducible diploma on page 247

Steps to Follow

1. Cover the bulletin board with the yellow butcher paper.

2. Make the graduate:
   - Cut a circle from the light brown paper for the head.
   - Cut strips of yarn for hair. Glue to the head.
   - Add facial features with black marking pen.

3. Cut a parallelogram of black paper for the mortarboard. Make a tassel of braided yarn and attach with a paper fastener.

4. Fold the black butcher paper in half and cut to make the robe.

5. Pin or staple the head, mortarboard, and robe in place.

6. Cut two small light brown circles for hands and pin them to the ends of the sleeves.

7. Roll a white sheet of copy paper into a tube to represent the diploma.

8. Cut two half circles for shoes. Pin in place.

9. Pin the caption to the board.

10. Pin up the students' diplomas (form on page 247).

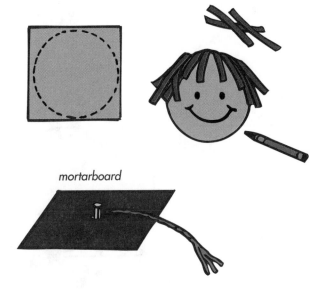

mortarboard

robe

hands   shoes

page 247

Congratulations

_____

on a job well done!

Congratulations

_____

on a job well done!

Graduation

Graduating doesn't always mean leaving high school or college. Discuss different times that students graduate to a new level or challenge. Write statements to validate the growth your students have made.

Jane graduated from addition to multiplication.

Peter graduated from paragraphs to research reports.

John graduated from picture books to novels.

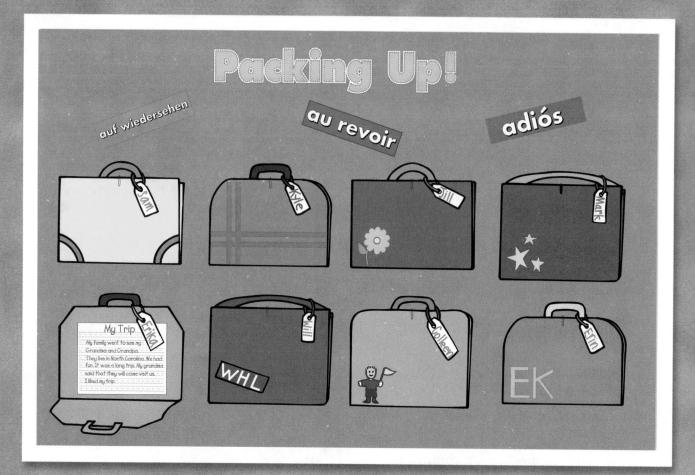

Packing Up!

Materials

- background—bright blue butcher paper
- suitcases—12″ x 18″ (30.5 x 45.5 cm) assorted colored construction paper
- suitcase handles—assorted colored construction paper scraps
- student writing paper
- tags—2″ x 4″ (5 x 10 cm) white construction paper
  string
  paper clips
- cutouts:
  caption letters on page 249, laminated and trimmed
  luggage tags on page 252, reproduced, laminated, and trimmed
  (Be sure to do this prior to cutting out the word strips on the other side of the page.)
  word strips on page 251, laminated and trimmed

Steps to Follow

1. Cover the bulletin board with the blue butcher paper and add the caption.

2. Have students make the suitcases.

   • Fold the construction paper in half.

   • Students may round corners or not. Each suitcase will be different.

   • Cut out a handle and glue it to the top back of the suitcase.

   • Draw details with marking pens.

3. Students write their names on the tags and punch a hole in them. Attach to the suitcase with a strip of string.

4. Staple student work inside the suitcases.

5. Pin the suitcases to the bulletin board. Secure the suitcases with paper clips to hold them shut.

6. Pin up the good-bye word strips.

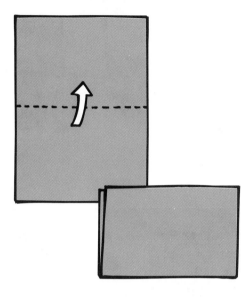

End of Year

If you were going to pack up special memories of your school year, what would you include? Have each student write a patterned response:

I'm packing up my memories.

I'm taking _____,

_____,

and _____.

I'm off to _____.

Glue the responses inside the suitcases.

SUMMER

C

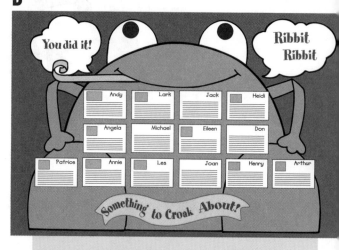

A

B

D

G

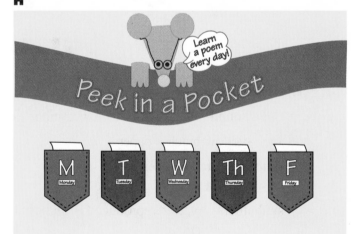

H

Summer Fun

Materials

- background—light blue, dark blue, and yellow butcher paper

- sun—yellow butcher paper

- umbrella—red butcher paper
        a piece of doweling

- sunbathers—pattern reproduced from pages 257 and 258
        crayons

- towels—12″ x 18″ (30.5 x 45.5 cm) white construction paper
        tempera paint in bright colors

- cutouts:
  caption letters on page 253 and 255, laminated and trimmed

Steps to Follow

1. Cover the bulletin board with butcher paper:

   • Cover the top half of the board with light blue butcher paper.

   • Cover the bottom half of the board with yellow butcher paper.

   • Add a strip of dark blue butcher paper in the center. Add wavy lines with a marking pen.

2. Cut out a large yellow sun from butcher paper and pin it in the upper left-hand corner. Add rays extending out.

3. Cut out an umbrella from the red butcher paper. Add details with a marking pen. Pin the umbrella to the board and add a piece of doweling as the pole.

4. Make sunbathers.

   • Reproduce the pattern on pages 257 and 258 for each student. Students cut out the body outlines, and then glue the two parts together. Have them use crayons to make a picture of themselves as a sunbather at the beach.

   • Students paint the white construction paper with bright primary colors to look like beach towels.

   • Glue the sunbather pictures to the towels.

5. Pin the towels on the board.

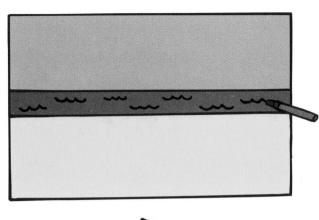

sun

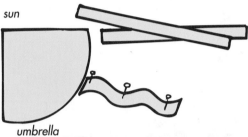

umbrella

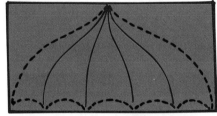

pages 257 and 258

Sun Couplets

Try writing sun couplets.

Radiant yellow, shining bright,
Rising sun turns off the night.

Hot spot in the sun.
Cool pool—we'll have fun.

Fishing for Good Work

Materials

- background—blue and yellow butcher paper

- boat—brown butcher paper

- fisherman:
  hat—9″ x 12″ (23 x 30.5 cm) red construction paper
  arm—4″ x 18″ (10 x 45.5 cm) blue construction paper
  hand—6″ x 6″ (15 x 15 cm) flesh-colored construction paper

- fishing rod:
  a piece of doweling
  string
  pipe cleaner

- cutouts:
  caption letters on pages 259 and 261, laminated and trimmed
  fish on page 263, laminated and trimmed

Steps to Follow

1. Cover the top half of the bulletin board with yellow butcher paper. Add a strip of blue to the bottom half. Scallop the top like waves.

2. Cut out a boat from brown butcher paper. Add details with a marking pen. Slip the boat behind the waves and pin in place.

3. Cut out the construction paper pieces for the fisherman as shown. Pin these pieces together in the boat.

4. Make the fishing rod.

   • Attach string to the end of the dowel.

   • Bend the pipe cleaner into a hook shape and attach it to the line. Pin the fishing rod to the board in the hand of the fisherman.

5. Pin the fish in the water.

6. Add student work.

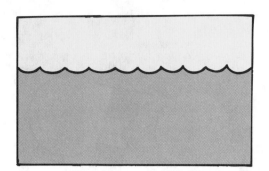

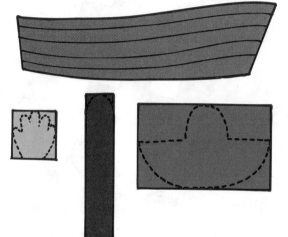

Evaluate Your Work

Have your students choose the work that is to be mounted on the board. They should complete a 3″ x 5″ note card that explains why they chose the example they did. Add your comment to the card. Mount the cards beside the work.

Name

What It Is

Why It's Good

Yum! What Good Work

Materials

- background—green butcher paper
- red and white checkered tablecloth (plastic, paper, or cloth)
- paper plates and napkins
- ruler
- red and black ants, reproduced from patterns on pages 267 and 270
- writing form for each student, reproduced from page 270
  (Be sure to do this prior to cutting out the sign on the other side.)
- cutouts:
  caption letters on pages 265 and 267, laminated and trimmed
  sign on page 269, laminated and trimmed

Steps to Follow

1. Cover the bulletin board with green butcher paper.

2. Pin the tablecloth diagonally across the board.

3. Glue completed writing forms inside the paper plates. Pin the paper plates and paper napkins to the cloth.

4. Add the caption to the board.

5. Pin the ants along the border of the board.

6. Tape the sign to a ruler. Pin it in the top corner of the board.

page 267

page 270

page 269

A Healthy Picnic

Reinforce healthy nutrition by having each student plan a picnic that includes a healthy variety of foods. Use the writing form to list the foods and then glue the form to the center of the paper plate.

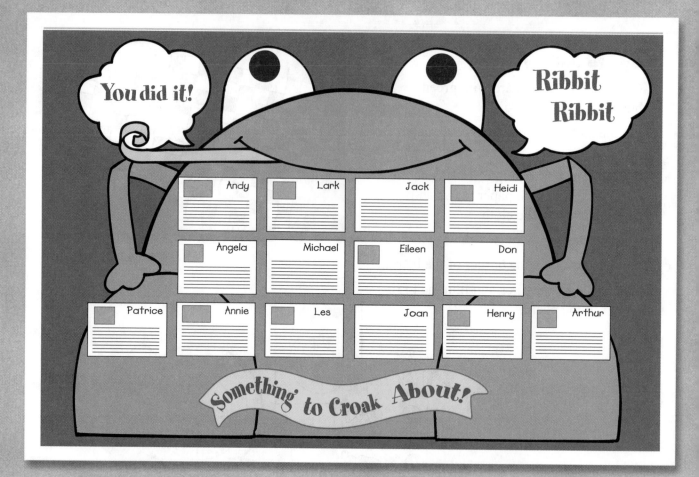

Something to Croak About!

Materials

- background—purple butcher paper
- frog:
  body–green butcher paper
  eyes—two 12″ x 18″ (30.5 x 45.5 cm) white construction paper
       two 4″ x 4″ (10 x 10 cm) black construction paper
  tongue—3″ x 18″ (7.5 x 45.5 cm) pink construction paper
- speech bubbles—two 12″ x 18″ (30.5 x 45.5 cm) white construction paper
- cutouts:
  banner and sentence strips on pages 271, 273, and 275, laminated and trimmed

Steps to Follow

1. Cover the bulletin board with purple butcher paper.

2. Make the frog.

   • Cut a large hill for the body. Make it as large as your board allows.

   • Cut two smaller hills for legs.

   • Pin the body to the board. Pin the legs on top of the body.

   • Cut two white hills for eyes. Glue a black circle on each eye. Add on top of the body.

   • Add a mouth with a marking pen.

   • Cut two arms from green paper. Pin them on the board, bend them over, and pin again.

   • Round one end of the tongue. Pin it in place on the board. Roll up the end.

3. Add the caption banner to the lower edge of the board.

4. Cut out the speech bubbles from white construction paper. Glue the message inside each bubble, and then pin them to the board.

5. Add student work.

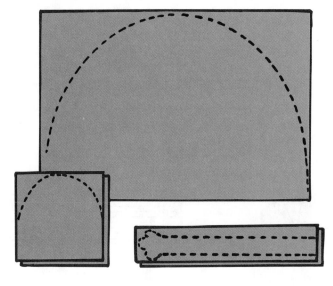

eyes

tongue

pages 271, 273, and 275

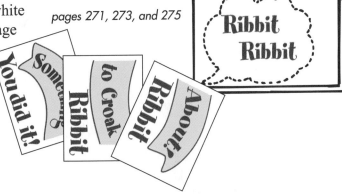

Ribbit Ribbit

Someone You did it!

Ribbit to Croak

About! Ribbit

Froggie

Long tongue, big eyes,

Loud croak, eats flies,

High jumps, webbed feet—

Proud pond athlete.

Just Ducky!

Materials

- background—yellow and blue butcher paper

- ducks:
  body—9″ x 12″ (23 x 30.5 cm) white construction paper
  head—6″ x 6″ (15 x 15 cm) white construction paper
  neck and wing—two 4″ x 6″ (10 x 15 cm) white construction paper
  beak—4″ x 8″ (10 x 20 cm) orange construction paper
  eyes—black beans or beads

- plants—green tissue paper

- cutouts:
  caption letters on pages 277, laminated and trimmed
  sentence strip on page 279, laminated and trimmed
  minnows on page 281, laminated and trimmed

Steps to Follow

1. Cover the top of the bulletin board with yellow butcher paper.

2. Cut a scalloped edge on the blue paper. Pin to the lower section of the board.

3. Make the ducks. For each duck:

   • Cut the body, head, neck, and wing out of white construction paper.

   • Use orange paper to create a beak.

   • Glue the body parts together to create different ducks.

4. Pin the ducks swimming in the water.

5. Cut water plants from green tissue paper. Pin them to the lower edge of the board.

6. Add the caption, minnows, and sentence strips.

7. The board is ready to display students' work.

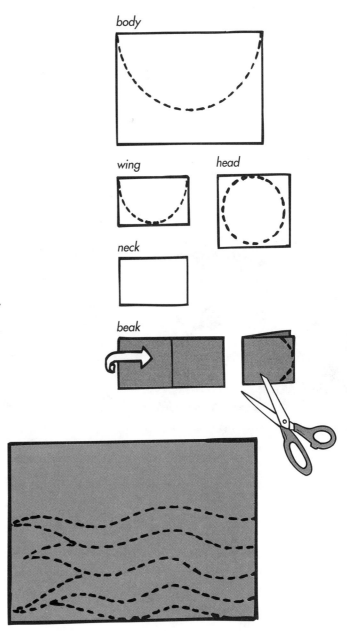

The Duck Parade

Mother Duck leads the parade.
    Quack, quack. Waddle, waddle.
Each fuzzy duckling is displayed.
    Quack, quack. Waddle, waddle.

They march along with head held high.
    Quack, quack. Waddle, waddle.
Nodding to each passerby.
    Quack, quack. Waddle, waddle.

Real Winners

Materials

- background—white butcher paper

- black and red construction paper squares 12″ x 12″ (30.5 x 30.5 cm)

- race car:
  body—brightly-colored foil wrapping paper
  tires—black construction paper and aluminum foil
  exhaust pipes—3 cardboard tubes and aluminum foil

- cutouts:
  caption letters on pages 283 and 285, laminated and trimmed
  driver on page 287, laminated and trimmed

Steps to Follow

1. Cover the top of the bulletin board with white butcher paper.

2. Fill the bottom part of the board with black and red checks.

3. Make the race car.

   • Cut out the race car from foil wrapping paper. Pin the car to the top edge of the checkered background.

   • Cut two wheels from black paper.

   • Add foil circles for lug nuts on the wheels.

   • Cover the cardboard tubes with foil and pin them in place as exhaust pipes.

   • Draw exhaust with a black marker.

4. Cut out the driver and pin him in the driver's seat.

5. Add the caption.

6. Display student work.

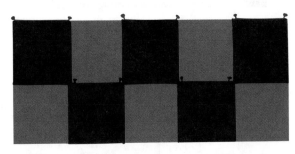

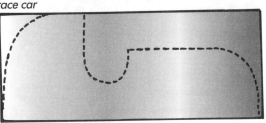

race car

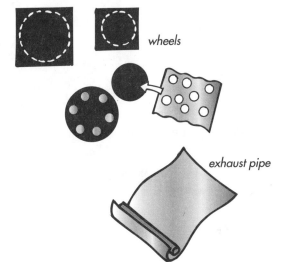

wheels

exhaust pipe

The Winners

Make ribbons to post with each piece of work displayed on the Real Winners board.

Cut a 3″ (7.5 cm) circle of colored paper.
Cut a 2″ (5 cm) circle of white paper.
Glue the white circle in the center of the colored paper.
Write the award on the white circle. *Winner! Neat Handwriting!*
Fold a 7″ (18 cm) strip of wide ribbon in half.
Tape it to the back of the circle.
Notch the ends of the ribbon.

Winner

Sniffing Out Good Work

Materials

- background—yellow butcher paper

- bloodhound:
  head—12″ x 18″ (30.5 x 45.5 cm) white construction paper
  snout—9″ x 12″ (23 x 30.5 cm) brown construction paper
  ears—two 9″ x 12″ (23 x 30.5 cm) brown construction paper
  paws—two 4″ x 6″ (10 x 15 cm) white construction paper
  nose—3″ x 3″ (7.5 x 7.5 cm) black construction paper
  tongue—2″ x 3″ (5 x 7.5 cm) pink construction paper
  collar—3″ x 12″ (7.5 x 30.5 cm) blue construction paper
  brown and black marking pens

- 9″ x 12″ (23 x 30.5 cm) blue construction paper for mounting student work

- cutouts:
  caption letters on pages 289, 291, and 293, laminated and trimmed
  sniff bubbles on page 293, laminated and trimmed

Steps to Follow

1. Cover the board with yellow butcher paper.

2. Make the bloodhound.

   - Cut the construction paper pieces as shown.

   - Glue the snout to the head. Glue the nose on next.

   - Draw eyes with the black marking pen on each side of the nose.

   - Make brown spots on the head and paws with the brown marking pen.

   - Glue on the ears, tongue, and collar.

   - Pin the dog to the board, with the ears flopping forward.

3. Add the caption letters.

4. Add student work framed in blue construction paper.

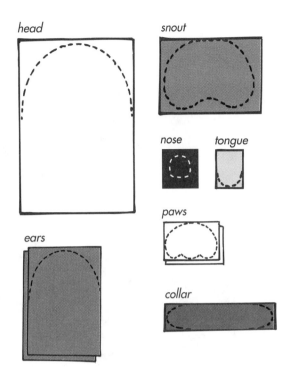

page 293

Dog Days of Summer

The period between July 3 and August 15 has been called "the dog days of summer" for thousands of years. The ancient Greeks and Romans noticed that the bright star Sirius (the Dog Star) rose around sunrise during this period. They believed the star added its heat to that of the sun, causing very hot weather.

Actually, it's hot in the Northern Hemisphere because the sun's rays hit the earth at a more direct angle.

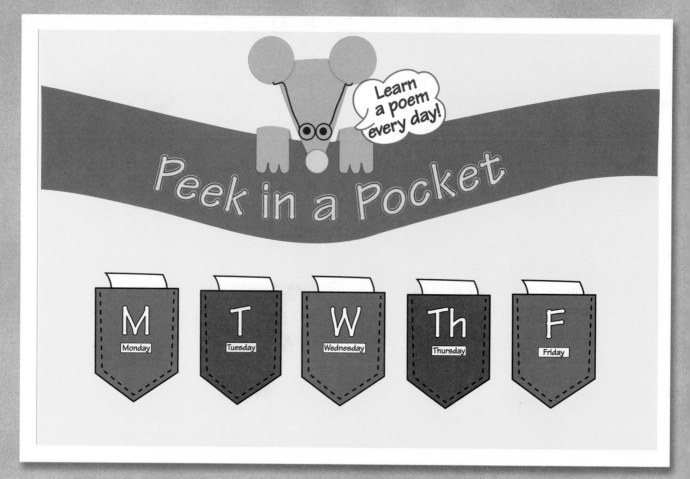

Peek in a Pocket

Materials

- background—yellow and red butcher paper

- pockets—9″ x 12″ (23 x 30.5 cm) red and blue construction paper

- poetry cards—5″ x 8″ (13 x 20 cm) file cards

- mouse:
  head—9″ x 12″ (23 x 30.5 cm) gray construction paper
  ears and paws—9″ x 12″ (23 x 30.5 cm) gray construction paper
  nose—3″ x 3″ (7.5 x 7.5 cm) square pink construction paper
  spectacles—2 black pipe cleaners

- cutouts:
  caption letters on pages 295 and 297, laminated and trimmed
  days of week letters and labels on pages 299 and 301, laminated and trimmed
  speech bubble on page 303, laminated and trimmed

Steps to Follow

1. Cover the bulletin board with the yellow butcher paper. Cut a red strip of butcher paper as a banner. Pin the caption letters to the banner

2. Make the mouse as shown.

    • Cut the gray construction paper for the head, ears, and paws.

    • Round the corners of the pink square of paper for the nose.

    • Twist the two pipe cleaners into spectacles. Add eyes with a black marker.

3. Make the pockets as shown.

    • Cut the blue and red construction paper in the pocket shape. Make stitches with the black marker.

    • Cut out the days of the week letters and labels and glue them on each pocket.

4. Pin the pockets to the board. Pin them so that the poem cards can be slipped easily in and out the top of the pocket.

5. Print poems on the file cards. Fill each pocket with a poem.

6. Each morning, read the poem for the day and encourage students to memorize the poems.

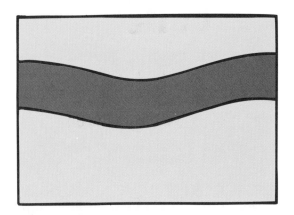

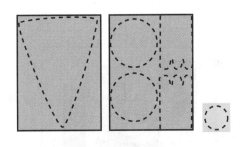

Other Functions

Change this board by changing the item in the pockets:

a joke	a story
a riddle	a job
a compliment	

Bulletin Board Cutouts

This book provides full-color cutouts to make creating bulletin boards easier for you. All cutouts should be

- removed from the book,

- laminated, and

- cut out.

Store your cutouts in an envelope paper-clipped to the direction pages. Since the letters and pictures are laminated, they can be used again and again.

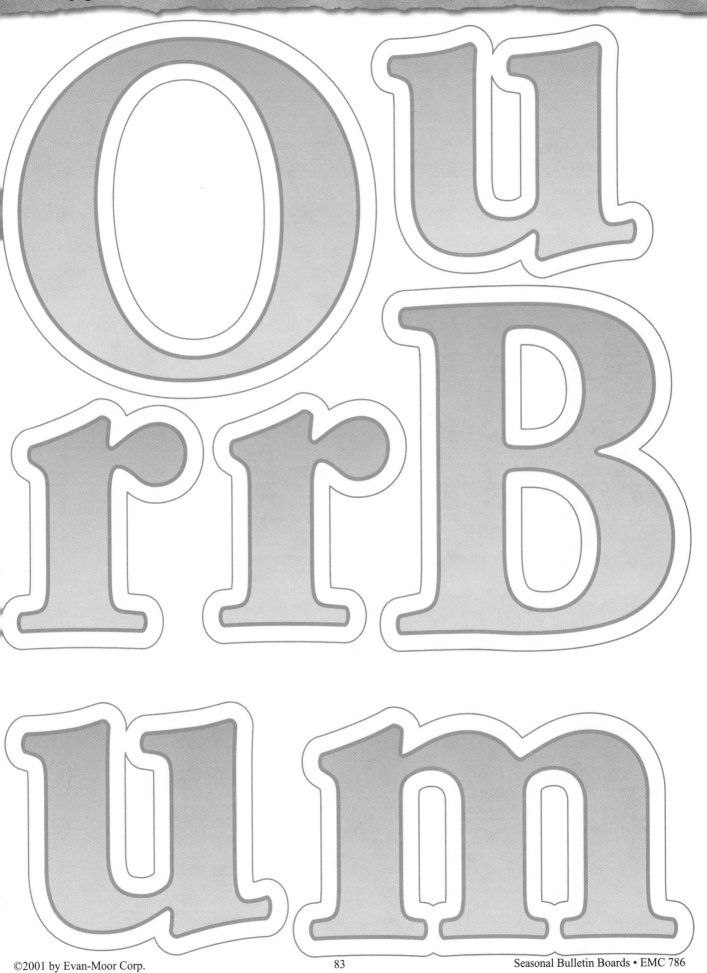

87

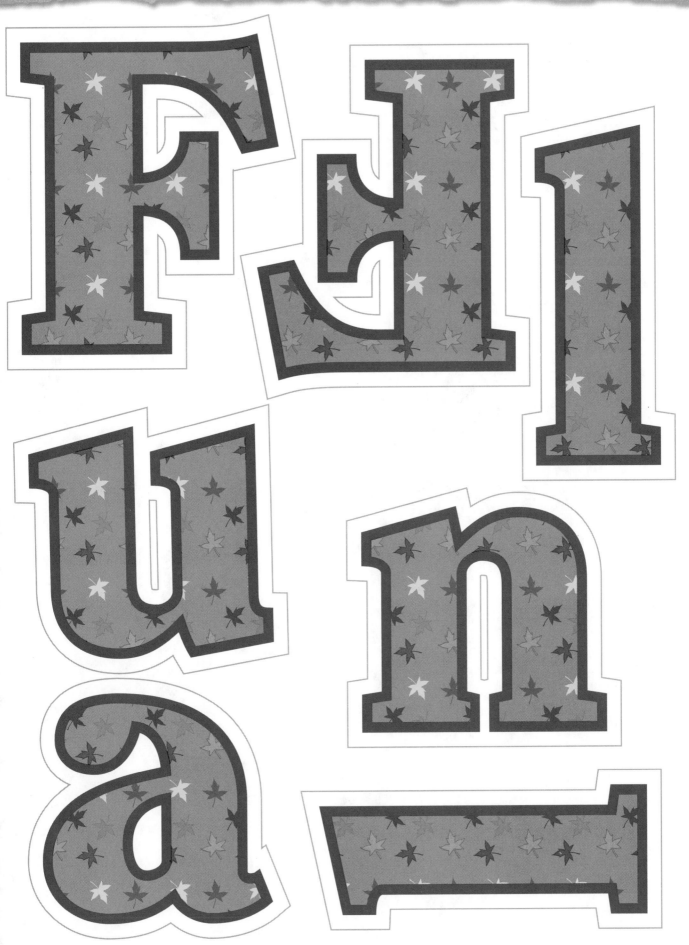

　　　　　　93

Apples

_____ , _____ , _____ , _____

_____ , _____ , _____

_____ , _____ , _____ , _____

_____ , _____ , _____

- -

Apples

_____ , _____ , _____ , _____

_____ , _____ , _____

_____ , _____ , _____ , _____

_____ , _____ , _____

Good work

comes in many

varieties.

P is for pick and patch
and pumpkin too.
With pride we post
perfect papers to view.

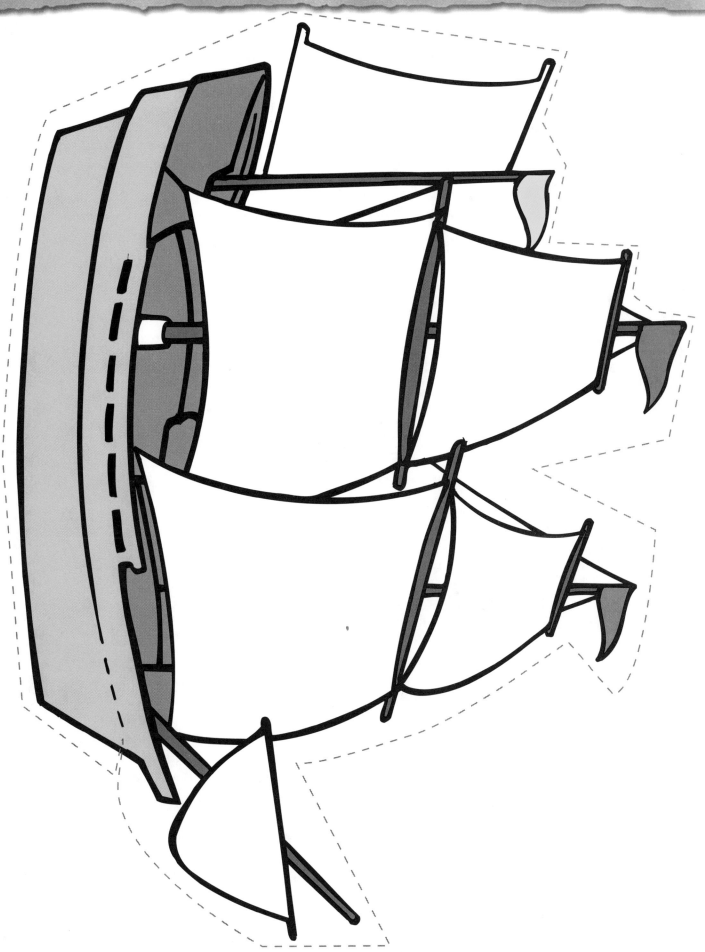

What are you Thankful for?

Seasonal Bulletin Boards • EMC 786

Where we walk to school each day

Indian children used to play—

What a different place today

Where we live and work and play!

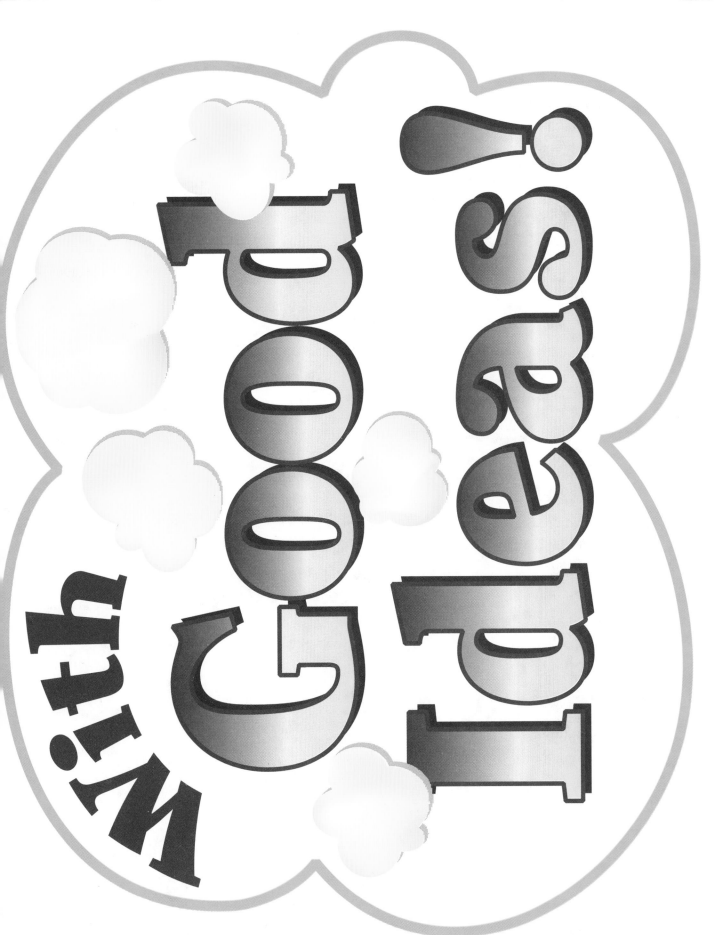

Seasonal Bulletin Boards • EMC 786

Seasonal Bulletin Boards • EMC 786

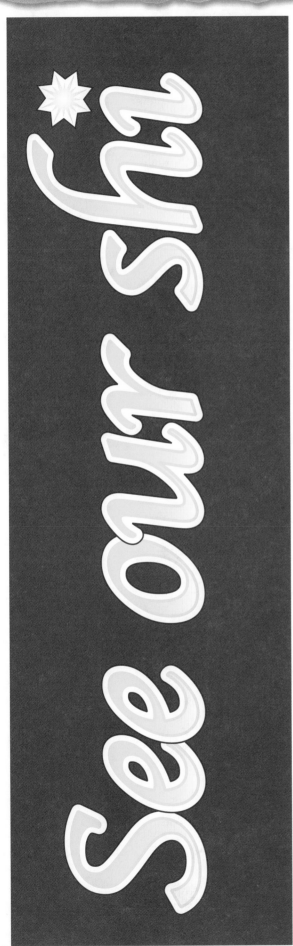

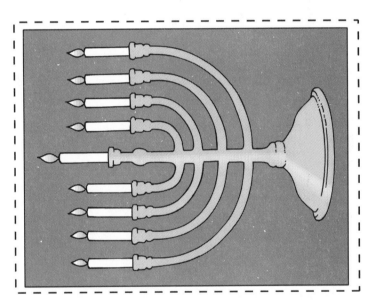

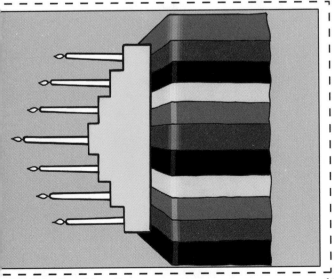

Christmas

Hanukkah

149

Kwanzaa

Las Posadas

December

SUNDAY	MONDAY	TUESDAY	WEDNESDAY	THURSDAY	FRIDAY	SATURDAY

Name _____

How Do You Celebrate?

Seasonal Bulletin Boards • EMC 786

Seasonal Bulletin Boards • EMC 786

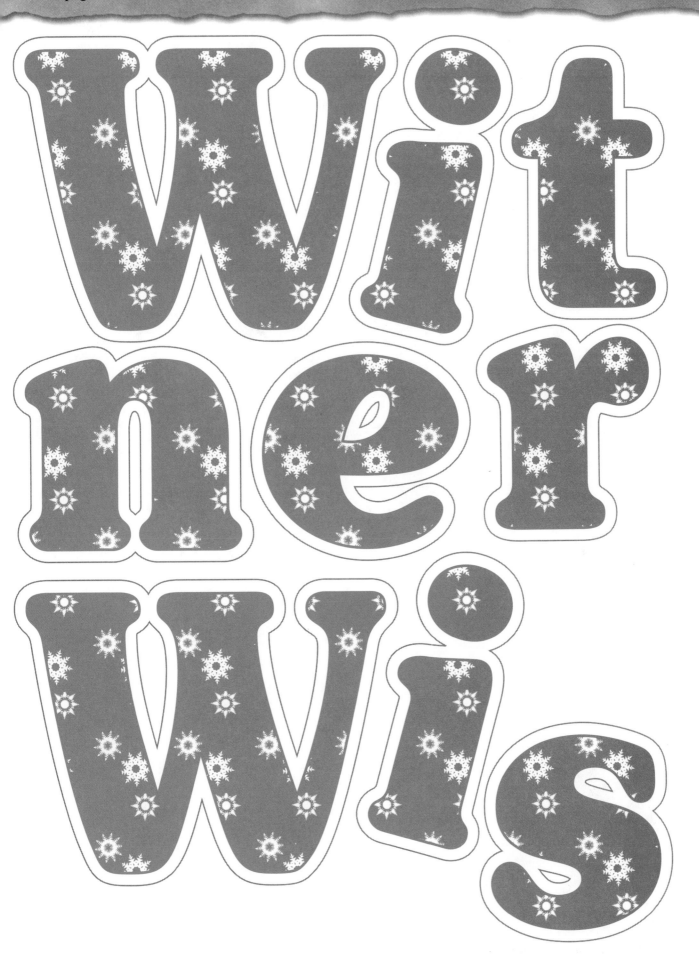

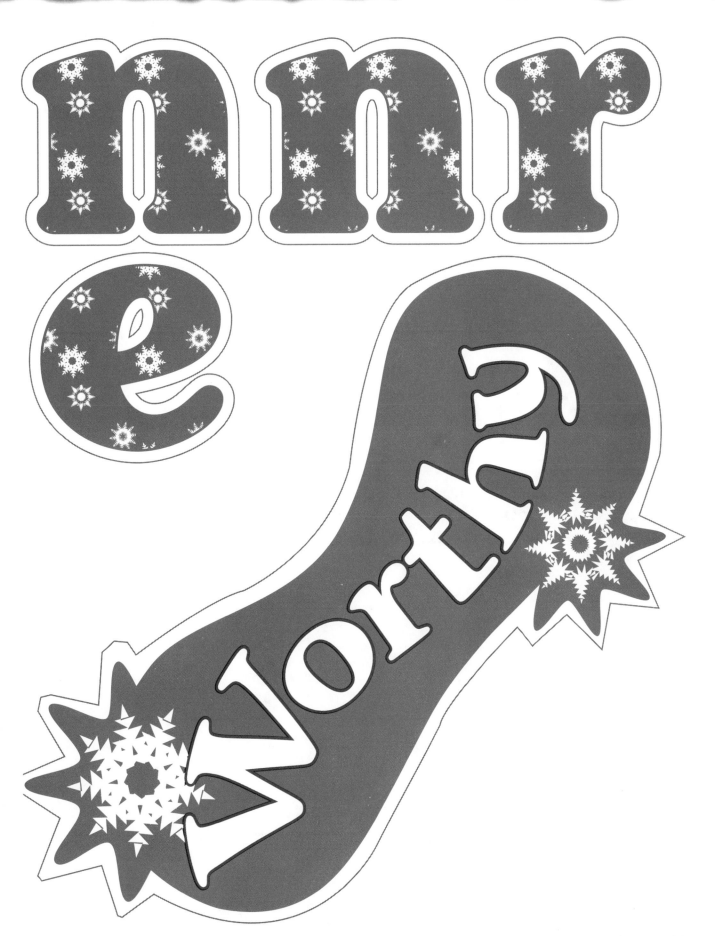

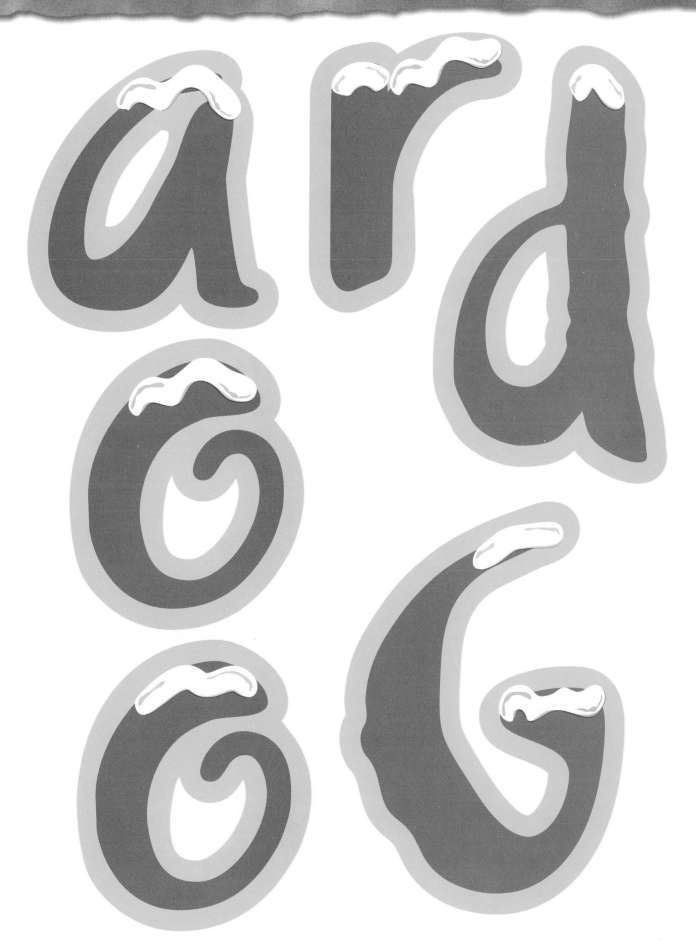